CW01496349

Carefree Campfire Cooking

Brenda Chase

PublishAmerica
Baltimore

First printing

At the specific preference of the author, PublishAmerica allowed this work to remain exactly as the author intended, verbatim, without editorial input.

ISBN: 1-4241-7838-X
PUBLISHED BY PUBLISHAMERICA, LLLP
www.publishamerica.com
Baltimore

Printed in the United States of America

Introduction

When I started going on camping trips with my own family it occurred to me that I was so busy attending to the tasks of the cooking chores that I no longer had the time that I once had as a child to enjoy the experience. Not having all the conveniences of home it seemed as though it didn't matter whether I was in a spacious RV, pick up camper or tent all I did was prepare, cook and clean up the daily meals for the entire trip.

Having a deep love for the rugged beauty of the wilderness and strongly wanting to experience it often without all of the extra work. I concluded that I must solve my dilemma while still providing the same type of experiences that I had enjoyed as a child for my own children. Keeping in mind that it is often the food on such a trip that we remember equally to the activities I began experimenting with different ways of preparing meals at camp that required the least amount of my time while still providing memorable experiences.

As I progressed in this adventure I found that camping became more carefree as I eliminated most of the hard and time consuming work giving myself more leisure time with my family.

After about twenty years or so I had a good collection of hearty down-home-cookin' recipes that were economical and easy to prepare.

So I put together a collection of my favorite camp fire recipes for any time of day and some helpful tips along with instructions and illustrations with hope that more people will have great experiences with nature as my family and I have had in the past.

I hope you find this book helpful and informative and I hope you enjoy the recipes too.

Table of Contents

Chapter One
Techniques

Some of you might be familiar with the following techniques for camp fire cooking. Therefore it is with those who might not be familiar with these techniques that I am describing the methods necessary to prepare the recipes in the following chapters.

The techniques described here are methods that have worked out very well for me in the past and hopefully will work out very well for you in your future. In time you too will be able to prepare hearty dishes and have allot more leisure time while in the outdoors as I have.

So let's move on to the basics. The camp fire will actually take the place of any camp stove you might have. Which means that if you are camping in a tent there will be one less thing to pack! However the portable camp stove can be convenient when you want hot water for a beverage or other reasons without building a campfire. The type (or shape) of fire that is needed depends on the cooking technique you are planning to use. There are many different ways to design a campfire pit. The two types that I regularly use are the standard round campfire as illustrated bellow and the keyhole shaped campfire as illustrated bellow.

Roundfire Pit

Keyhole Fire Pit

The standard round fire pit that we are all familiar with has allot of cooking uses: foil cooking, can cooking, clothes hanger cooking, and of course, cooking on a stick. If cooking on the fire is intended the fire pit will need to be dug approximately 4' to 5' across and approximately 18" deep. After this is accomplished line the perimeter with rocks to help contain the fire within the pit.

When a less direct heat is needed for foods that would burn before it is done in the center such as one pot meals, muffins, biscuits, and some desserts the keyhole shaped fire pit is essential.

The keyhole fire pit is simply a round fire pit with a 12" to 18" square dug approximately 4" to 6" deep in one end and also lined with rocks like the round end where a rack (an old oven rack works best) is placed for cooking. Try to find rocks that are close to the same size for the square end so the cooking rack is as level as possible when in place for cooking.

It will take some time to build up 2" to 3" of hot coals in the fire pit needed for cooking in the coals. Adding charcoal briquettes speeds up the process quite a bit and the charcoal lasts much longer than wood coals so replenishing the coals isn't necessary as often. Using lighter fluid for the charcoal briquettes can be done but it is not nessesary. Smaller sticks will make coals faster because they burn faster. The more coals that are accumulated the hotter your cooking fire will be. Adding charcoal briquettes will also increase the cooking temperature varying depending on the amount added. The more charcoal briquettes you add the higher the cooking temperature will be. I usually work with a mixture of about 25% charcoal and 75% wood coals. It is for this reason that all times indicated for the recipes in this book are approximate. Of course if you are cooking on the rack or a stick you can get away with a much smaller accumulation of hot coals saving some time.

A shovel will need to be kept near the fire so that you can move fresh coals where needed during cooking and of course in case the fire gets out of control…after all you are burning dry fuel which is all around your camp!! I even keep a bucket of water near by. I don't want to be responsible for burning down the very wilderness that I came to enjoy and I would like the opportunity to come back again! A small fold up shovel or fireplace tool shovel is nice when you need to place a small amount of coals on top of the double pan because you have more control over the shovel.

Foil cooking is the method that I use most often because the food doesn't require as much attention while cooking. A good quality heavy duty aluminum foil is a must.

For the standard foil method: Step #1: Tear off a piece of foil about 3 times wider than the food to be cooked. **Step #2:** Spray the non-shiny side of the foil with a non-stick cooking spray. **Step #3:** Lay the food in the center of the foil. **Step #4:** Bring up the sides of the foil so that they are together. **Step #5:** Fold down approximately 1 1/2" of the foil; repeat again making a double fold. **Step #6:** Fold up the ends of the foil in the same manner as the sides making sure that they are folded up…not down. (illustration#1) This keeps juices in the foil so that the food doesn't dry out or burn. **Step #7:** Pierce a small hole in one side of the foil with a small knife or fork to allow the steam to escape. *Always pierce a small hole in the side of the foil unless recipe specifies otherwise.* **Step #8:** Lay the foil wrapped food directly on the hot coals and cook according to the recipe. For foods that require more than a half an hour cooking time coals will need to be replenished by scooping some new ones from a small fire kept burning in the side of the fire pit and placing them in the cooking area a few times. The top fold of the foil makes a good"handle" to grab with a pair of tongs when removing food from the fire. Always place foil wrapped food on a tray or cutting board to carry to the table as they can break open resulting in a possible injury.

Illustration 1

For the open foil method: This method is used for foods that are turned over or stirred while cooking. **Step #1:** Tear off a piece of foil 3 times larger than the food. **Step #2:** Spray the non-shiny side of the foil with a non-stick cooking spray. **Step #3:** Lay the food in the center and fold the sides and ends of the foil up about 1½" two times leaving the top open. This forms a pan of sorts. (illustration # 2) **Step #4:** Lay the food in the foil directly on the hot coals or on the rack over the square end of the keyhole fire pit. Cook according to the recipe directions.

Illustration # 2

For dense foods such as a potato: **Step #1:** Tear off a piece of foil large enough to wrap all the way around the food overlapping at least 2".**Step #2:** Place food in the center of the foil and roll up in the foil. **Step #3:** Twist the ends of the foil. (illustration #3) **Step #4:** Place directly on hot coals and cook according to the recipe.

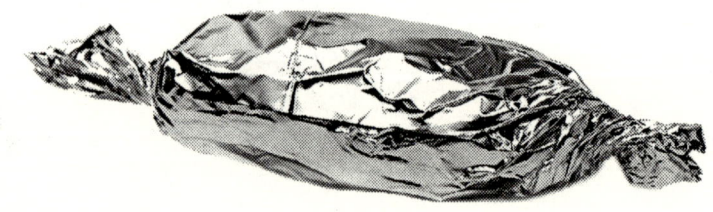

Illustration # 3

To make a teepee style foil pan: Step #1: Tear off a piece of foil big enough to form over your fist plus about 6" to 8" extra. Once formed around the fist flatten the bottom. (illustration #4) **Step #2:** Add the ingredients. **Step #3:** Place directly on the hot coals and cook according to the recipe.

Illustration # 4

To make a clothes hanger griddle / frying pan: Step #1: Using a *wire* clothes hanger grasp the hook and the center of the side opposite from the hook and pull to form a square. **Step #2:** Turn the hook up to form a handle. (illustration #5) **Step #3:** Cover the square part of the hanger with a double layer of foil. (illustration #6) Use according to the recipe.

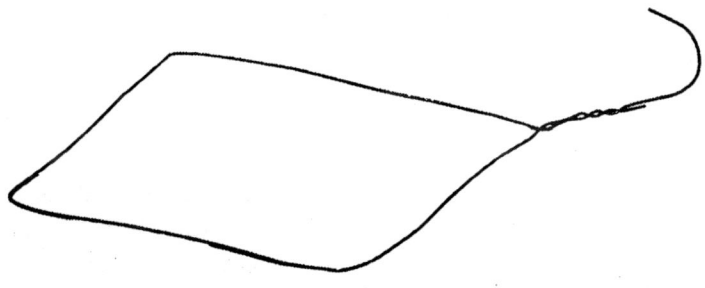

Illustration # 5

Illustration # 6

Cooking on a stick: I think everyone is familiar with cooking hot dogs or marshmallows on a stick over the fire. There is a good variety of metal sticks for this purpose that can be purchased. If you are going to cut your own from willows make sure that the wood is green (meaning it is still alive and flexible) and peel the bark from the end that the food will be on. Dry willows will catch fire.

Cooking dough on a stick: The canned variety of dough (biscuits, cinnamon rolls, bread sticks ect…) is what you need to work with to cook dough on a stick. The cheaper types will stay on the stick better because the flakier moister types have enough moisture that they sort of melt off from the stick while cooking over the coals. Also the canned cinnamon rolls that are factory cut into a strip and then rolled into a spiral work better than the cinnamon rolls that are in the shape of a biscuit when they come out of the can because they are easier to wrap around the stick. Do not hold dough directly over an open flame as this will result in a burnt crust and raw middle. Each biscuit will need to be worked in the hand to slightly warm it and mold it from a round into a strip. Then wrap the strip in a spiral fashion around the stick and pinch the seams together tight enough to hold the dough together during cooking. (Illustration # 7) Dough needs a longer cooking time and less direct heat than a meat product so it will need to be held about 6" or 7" above the coals rotating the stick as the dough browns until all of the sides of the dough is browned and the middle is cooked through. Then simply slide the dough off the end of the stick.

Illustration #7

Cooking other foods on a stick: Hold the stick with the food on it approximately 3" from the heat rotating as necessary. Stick cooking can be done over an open flame but coals work better resulting a slow roasted flavor.

Double pan method: At times you might want to make something that is a little more delicate like muffins or something that requires allot of stirring or a one pot meal that includes a sauce or gravy. This is where the double pan method comes in. **Step #1:** Spray one 8" foil disposable round or square cake pan with a non-stick cooking spray. **Step #2:** Add the ingredients. **Step #3:** Cover the bottom pan that has the food in it with foil if specified or a second foil pan turned upside down and secure the pans together with 3 or 4 medium size (about 1") metal binder clips or 2" metal alligator clips. (illustration # 8) Clothes pins can be used but they will eventually burn. Cook according to the recipe. Remove the clips using oven mitts.

Illustration # 8

Chapter Two
Equipment and Tips

It doesn't matter whether you are going camping in a tent or an RV everyone could use a little extra space from time to time. And knowing how to keep the dust out of things can come in handy too! Because I rarely use pots and pans for cooking when I go camping I only need to pack a coffee pot and a couple of small sauce pots with lids in case I have a need for hot water for something. This saves space no matter what I'm camping in.

Pack things inside other things: Hot pads, oven mitts, hand towels, cocoa mix, coffee and sugar (packed in re-closeable sandwich bags) can all fit into the coffee pot and pans. Pots and pans should have metal instead of plastic handles so that they don't melt or burn. Cast iron is great but it is heavy and is not necessary.

Coolers: If you are using coolers having two is a good idea … one for food and one for beverages so the food cooler doesn't get opened as often. This helps the food stay cold and the ice last longer.

Campfire soot on pans: To keep the stubborn black soot off of your metal pots and pans that comes from cooking on the fire rub the outside of the pan with a thin layer of dish soap before use (not cast iron—soap will rust them) and leave it on until you are finished with the pan or pot and then wipe the dish soap and the soot off with a few wet paper towels. This works wonderful and your pots and pans will be clean of all soot with out scrubbing!!

Transporting eggs: Whether in a cooler, ice box or refrigerator it can be a disaster! Especially when you get to your destination and find pre-scrambled eggs complete with the shells!! The solution is an easy one. Break the eggs open into an opened re-closeable plastic bag. Be careful not to stir or break the yolks and carefully squeeze out the air and seal the bag. Place the bag full of eggs into a suitable sized plastic container with a lid if desired. Pack them into the cooler or refrigerator. When you are ready to use the eggs open the re-closeable bag about half way and holding in both hands tilt the bag at an angle towards the cooking surface holding the bag so that the opened part remains open and they will pour out unbroken one at a time!!

Ice in a jug: Instead of buying bags of blocked ice for the cooler or ice box and then having it melt all over everything making a huge mess and ruining certain types of food save your empty gallon milk jugs and wash them thoroughly. Then fill them ¾ full of cold water and replace the lid and freeze. Place one or two frozen jugs in a large cooler instead of the bagged ice and as the ice melts you will have safe extra drinking water. The cooler is easier to clean at the end of the trip too! Ice in a jug lasts a little longer than the bagged blocked ice and if you save the jugs you will have them for the next trip.

Plastic bags: I think the re-closeable plastic bag is a great invention! The sandwich size is what I use the most for transporting food and other items to take camping. But there are allot of uses for the other sizes as well. For example a gallon sized bag can be used for a mixing bowl if you are careful not to tear the bag and some ingredients can just be shaken together instead of stirred after closing the bag such as a cake or muffin mix. But I think one of my favorites is the buttermilk biscuits as instructed later in this book. You can transport, mix, roll, and cut them right in the bag! When silverware, napkins, tooth brushes, and coffee filters are sealed in a bag it keeps the dust off during travel. There seems to be never ending uses for these convenient little plastic bags when it comes to camping!

Disposable measuring cup: An 8oz paper or plastic disposable cup can be used. A line can be drawn on the outside of the cup with a marker at ½, ¼, and ¾ intervals and filled to the needed mark for ½ cup, ¼ cup and ¾ cup measurements. There are 8oz in one cup so other sized cups can be used as well: 6oz = ¾ cup, 12oz = 1¼ cups and 16oz = 2 cups.

Keeping travel dust out: If you have a problem with heavy road dust getting into the drawers in your RV you can remove the drawer and slip a kitchen sized garbage bag over the drawer. Then replace the drawer with the bag wrapped around it. Remove the bag when your destination is reached and the entire drawer and its contents will be clean!

Equipment: The basic equipment that you will need to prepare the recipes in this book are minimal.

Tin foil: When it comes to choosing a heavy duty tin foil get a good brand. The less expensive brands are not thick enough to prevent food from burning. Cook with the shiny side of the foil away from the food and toward the fire because the shiny side reflects heat and the non-shiny side absorbs heat. This helps to prevent the heat from becoming to intense and burning the food.

Tongs: A good quality long handled set of tongs are indispensable. The tongs made for the barbecue is a good choice. To keep the tongs from springing open during travel wrap a twist tie around the grabbing end and they can then be placed in an empty cardboard paper towel core to keep them under control.

Oven mitts and hot pads: Two oven mitts will be required for reaching into the fire to check or retrieve food. Even with a pair of long tongs the intense heat from the fire can burn the skin without coming into contact with the fire itself. A hot pad might come in handy for the coffee pot or a pan with a handle so it's a good idea to include at least one incase it's needed.

Spices and seasonings: These can be packed into plastic spice bottles. To keep them together during travel put them in a plastic re-closeable bag.

Dishes and utensils: I never use regular plates or silverware because I don't have to wash a paper plate. However I usually carry a few regular plates and some silverware incase I run out of the paper types. I never wash a paper plate. I feel that if I am spending the money on a paper plate it is because I don't want to wash dishes and if I wash the paper plate then I've wasted my money because I already own plates that have to be washed!! For emergency dishes I usually carry four or five each: plates, metal teaspoons, forks, tablespoons, butter knives, steak knives, coffee cups and beverage cups. Even if you plan to use paper plates and plastic silverware you will still need to keep on hand a turner, tongs, wire whip, cutting knives, cutting board, measuring spoons and steak knives for cooking. You can place the dirty non-disposable utensils in a used gallon sized re-closeable bag and wash them when you get home it's still better than washing dishes in camp!

Miscellaneous: A small plastic bottle of dish soap (not to wash dishes of course!) to rub on pots and pans, a couple of hand towels, a dish cloth (for wiping off the table), a good first aid kit, a roll of paper towels (or two if you are going to roast corn), a good hand can opener, non-stick cooking spray, a cooking rack (I use an old oven rack), 5 to 10 gallons of water, a bar of soap and a couple of wash cloths and of course … this book.

Transporting sharp knives: An empty potato chip can is very effective. Just place the knives handle side facing up into the empty can and close the lid. If there is a knife that is to long for one of these cans a sheath can be made by flattening an empty paper towel roll and wrapping the empty roll with duct tape.

Chapter Three
Foil Cooking

Ease of preparation combined with no clean up makes this method convenient and versatile.

Lemon Chicken Breasts page 31

Fiesta Chicken

2 cups salsa
1 Tablespoon dry mustard
3 Tablespoons brown sugar
1 Tablespoon cumin
4 skinless boneless chicken breasts
6 ounces cheddar cheese, shredded
Sour cream

Prepare ahead: Place chicken breasts into a re-closeable bag and seal. In a separate bag mix salsa, brown sugar, dry mustard and cumin and seal the bag.
At camp: Using the standard foil method place the chicken breasts onto a piece of prepared foil. Cover each chicken breast with the salsa mixture lifting each chicken breast to allow the sauce to run underneath the chicken breasts. Wrap and lie the pouches onto the hot coals. Cook for approximately 10 to 15 minutes or until chicken breasts are no longer pink. Open foil and cover with the shredded cheese and reclose the pouches. Place each pouch on the edge of the hot coals for 5 minutes or until cheese is melted. Top with sour cream if desired.
Serves 4

Italian Chicken and Potatoes

4 boneless skinless chicken breasts
2 Tablespoons Italian seasoning
1 pound baby red potatoes
½ teaspoon garlic salt
3 Tablespoons flour
1½ cups Italian salad dressing
1¾ cups dry parmesan cheese (optional)

Prepare ahead: Place chicken breasts into a gallon re-closeable bag and sprinkle with one Tablespoon of Italian seasoning and seal the bag. In a separate smaller re-closeable bag combine Italian salad dressing, flour and parmesan cheese and seal the bag. Shake vigorously to mix ingredients.

At camp: Using the standard foil method place each chicken breast onto a piece of prepared foil. Cut the potatoes into ½" cubes and divide into four servings. Place each serving on a piece of prepared foil next to a chicken breast. Sprinkle each serving of potatoes with ½ teaspoon of Italian seasoning and ¼ teaspoon of garlic salt. Pour the dressing mixture evenly over the chicken and the potatoes. Wrap and lie the pouches onto the hot coals and cook for approximately 20 minutes or until potatoes are tender. Check the potatoes for tenderness after 10 minutes.

Serves 4

Barbecued Chicken

1 whole thawed cut-up fryer chicken
1-10 ounce bottle barbecue sauce

Prepare ahead: Remove skin from the chicken pieces. Place the chicken pieces on a microwave safe plate and cover it with a paper towel. Microwace on high for approximately 7 to 10 minutes or until chicken is half cooked. Cool the chicken and put it into a re-closeable gallon bag. Pour the barbecue sauce over the chicken in the bag and seal.

At camp: Using the open foil method place all of the chicken on a single large piece of prepared foil. Lie the chicken in the open foil onto the hot coals and pour the barbecue sauce from bag over the chicken turning to coat the pieces. Cook 5 minutes. Turn and cook 5 to 7 more minutes or until cooked through.

Serves 4

Bacon Swiss Chicken Rolls

4 boneless skinless chicken breasts; thawed
4 thin slices ham
8 thin bacon strips
4 thin slices Swiss cheese

Prepare ahead: With a meat mallet pound the chicken to ½"
thickness and pat each breast dry on both sides with paper towels.
Place one slice of ham and one slice of Swiss cheese on each chicken
breast. Roll up each breast tucking in the ends. In a spiral fashion
wrap two pieces of bacon around each rolled breast over lapping
bacon slightly to allow for shrinking. Wrap each rolled chicken
breast in plastic wrap and place all of the wrapped breasts into a re-
closeable bag and seal.

At camp: Remove the chicken rolls from the plastic wrap. Using the
standard foil method place each of the chicken rolls in the center of
a piece of prepared foil. Wrap like a baked potato: *do not pierce a
hole in the foil.* Lie the pouches onto the hot coals. Cook for 20
minutes, turning one quarter turn every 5 minutes or until chicken is
no longer pink.

* *Variations: Finely chopped broccoli and American cheese or
cream cheese and finely chopped thawed frozen spinach can be used
in place of the ham and the Swiss cheese.*

Serves 4

Chicken and Peppers

1½ pounds uncooked chicken tenders
1 Tablespoon garlic powder
1 Tablespoon onion powder
1½ teaspoons seasoned salt
1 teaspoon parsley flakes
½ teaspoon paprika
1 green bell pepper
1 red bell pepper
8 ounces small whole mushrooms
Cooking oil

Prepare ahead: Place the chicken tenders into a re-closeable bag and sprinkle with the garlic powder, seasoned salt, paprika, onion powder, and parsley flakes and seal the bag.

At camp: Divide the chicken into four servings. Using the standard foil method pour about 2 Tablespoons of oil in each of the four prepared pieces of foil. Place the chicken in the center of each piece of foil. Cut both of the peppers into ½" by 2" pieces. Divide the peppers into four servings and place into the foil pieces with the chicken and add washed mushrooms. Wrap the pouches and lie on the hot coals and cook for 10 to 15 minutes or until the peppers are tender.

Serves 4

Campfire Wings

2 pounds chicken wings
½ teaspoon cumin
1-7 ounce bottle taco sauce
¼ teaspoon minced garlic
½ cup water
1 teaspoon salt

Prepare ahead: Separate all of the chicken wings at the joints with a sharp knife discarding the wing tips. Place the chicken wing pieces into a re-closeable bag. Combine the remaining ingredients and pour over the wing pieces and seal the bag.
At camp: Using the standard foil method place all of the chicken wing pieces and the sauce into the center of one large piece of prepared foil. Wrap and lie the pouch onto the hot coals and cook for 15 to 20 minutes or until the chicken wings are tender. If necessary open the foil and leave them on the hot coals and let the sauce caramelize turning the chicken wing pieces often.
Serves 4

Lemon Chicken Breasts

4 boneless skinless chicken breasts
1-10 ounce bottle lemon flavor marinade sauce*

Prepare ahead: Place the chicken and the marinade together into a re-closeable bag and seal.

At camp: Using the standard foil method place each chicken breast onto a piece of prepared foil. Cover each chicken breast with the marinade sauce. Wrap the pouches and lie them onto the hot coals and cook for 10 to 15 minutes or until the chicken breats are no longer pink.

Variations: Any flavor of marinade can be used.

Serves 4

Saucy Stuffed Chicken Breasts

4 boneless, skinless chicken breasts
1-10 ounce can condensed
1¼ cups chicken flavored stuffing mix
cream of celery soup
1 Tablespoon Worcestershire sauce
½ cup water
¾ cup additional water

Prepare ahead: Place the chicken breasts into a re-closeable bag and seal.
At camp: Cut a pocket into each chicken breast not quite cutting all the way through the breast. Combine the stuffing mix and the ½ cup of water. Toss to coat the stuffing crumbs. Stuff each chicken breast with ¼ cup to ½ cup of the stuffing mixture. Using the standard foil method place each chicken breast onto the center of a piece of prepared foil.
Combine the condensed soup, the ¾ cup of water and the Worcestershire sauce and pour over the chicken breasts. Wrap the pouches and lie them onto the hot coals and cook for 10 to 15 minutes or until chicken is no longer pink.
Serves 4

Corned Beef 'n Cabbage

2-12 ounce cans corned beef
1 small head cabbage
4 cups water

At camp: Using the standard foil method open and cut the canned corned beef into four pieces. Cut the cabbage into eight wedges and remove the core and a few of the outer leaves. On each piece of prepared foil place one piece of the corned beef and two of the cabbage wedges. Pour 1 cup of water over the cabbage in each foil pouch. Wrap the pouches. *Do not pierce hole in foil.* Lie the pouches onto the hot coals and cook for 15 minutes. Turn the entire contents of the pouches over and cook another 15 minutes.
Serves 4

Marinated Top Sirloin Steak

4 top sirloin steaks cut ½" thick
¼ cup Worcestershire sauce
garlic salt
unseasoned meat tenderizer

Prepare ahead: Trim the fat from the edges of the steaks. Sprinkle each side of each steak with the meat tenderizer and the garlic salt using the garlic salt sparingly. Place all of the steaks into a re-closeable bag. Add the Worcestershire sauce and seal the bag. Shake the bag to distribute the ingredients.
At camp: Using the standard foil method place each steak onto a piece of prepared foil. Pour any remaining sauce over the steaks. Wrap the pouches, pierce a small hole in the side and lie the pouches onto the hot coals and cook for approximately 10 to 18 minutes or until the steasks are done as desired. Serve with steak sauce or horseradish.
Serves 4

Orange Steak

4 eye of round steaks cut 1" thick
1 cup orange juice
Unseasoned meat tenderizer
¼ teaspoon pepper
1 teaspoon garlic salt
¼ cup cooking oil
3 Tablespoons vinegar
1 teaspoon dry mustard

Prepare ahead: Sprinkle the meat tenderizer on each side of the steaks. Place the steaks into a re-closeable bag. Add the remaining ingredients and seal the bag. Shake the bag gently to mix the marinade.

At camp: Place each steak onto a prepared piece of foil. Pour the marinade sauce over the steaks. Wrap the pouches and pierce a small hole in the side. Lie the pouches onto the hot coals and cook 10 to 15 minutes.

Serves 4

Barbeque Ribs

1½ pounds boneless beef or pork ribs
1 teaspoon garlic salt
1-12 ounce bottle barbeque sauce
1 Tablespoon dry mustard
1 Tablespoon onion powder
1 Tablespoon unseasoned meat tenderizer

Prepare ahead: Place thawed ribs into a large kettle or skillet and add just enough water to cover the ribs. Bring to a boil and reduce the heat. Cover and simmer over medium low heat for 30 minutes. Remove the ribs from the liquid. Cool and place into a large re-closeable bag and add meat tenderizer, garlic salt, onion powder, and dry mustard. Seal the bag and shake it to distribute the seasonings.
At camp: Using the standard foil method place all of the ribs in a single layer onto a large piece of prepared foil and pour barbeque sauce over ribs turning to coat all sides of the ribs. Wrap the pouch and lie directly onto the hot coals for 15 to 20 minutes. Open the foil pouch and continue cooking the ribs turning occasionally until sauce caramelizes.
Serves 4

Stuffed Bell Peppers

2 green bell peppers
1 pound ground beef
½ small onion, chopped
1 teaspoon garlic powder
1 teaspoon onion powder
1 teaspoon seasoned salt
½ cup fine dry bread crumbs
1 egg
¼ cup ketchup

Prepare ahead: Mix all of the ingredients *except* the bell peppers. Put the mixed ingredients into a re-closeable bag and seal. Cut thin ends off of the stem end of the peppers and remove the membranes. Cut the peppers in half lengthwise. Wash and place the peppers into a separate bag and seal.

At camp: Divide the beef mixture into four servings and mold each serving into a bell pepper half. Using the standard foil method place each stuffed pepper onto a piece of prepared foil *meat side down.* Pour ½ cup water into each foil pouch with the stuffed peppers. Wrap but *do not pierce a hole in the foil* and lie the pouches onto the hot coals. Cook for 30 minutes. Open the foil and turn the stuffed peppers over and pour 2 Tablespoons of ketchup over the meat side of each stuffed pepper leaving the foil open and cook for another 5 minutes to warm the ketchup.

*Variation: If using cheese sauce instead of ketchup: eliminate the last 5 minutes and pour hot cheese sauce (instructions on page 97) over the stuffed peppers.

Serves 4

Soft Flour Tacos

1 pound ground beef
1 teaspoon season salt
¼ teaspoon pepper
1 teaspoon cumin
½ small chopped onion
1 teaspoon garlic powder
8-12" flour tortillas
1 teaspoon onion powder
shredded cheese
2 chopped tomatoes
shredded lettuce
hot sauce
sour cream

At camp: Using the open foil method crumble the ground beef onto a piece of prepared foil. Add the chopped onion and sprinkle with seasoned salt, cumin, garlic powder, onion powder, and pepper. Lie the foil with the ingredients onto the hot coals and cook stirring occasionally until done for about 5 minutes. Serve on tortillas and top with tomatoes, cheese and lettuce. Pass the hot sauce and sour cream.
Serves 4

Italian Beefwiches

1 pound ground beef
¼ cup water
1-1 ounce envelope dry Italian dressing mix
4 slices mozzarella cheese
8 hamburger buns
lettuce and sliced tomatoes

At camp: Using the open foil method crumble the ground beef onto a large piece of prepared foil and place onto the hot coals and cook stirring often until browned for about 5 minutes. Add the water and the dry Italian dressing mix and stir. Heat through. Serve on buns with cheese, lettuce and tomatoes.
Serves 4

Campfire Joes

1 pound ground beef
½ Tablespoon prepared mustard
½ Tablespoon vinegar
½ small onion chopped
½ teaspoon salt
¼ teaspoon pepper
2 Tablespoons sugar
¼ teaspoon chili powder
½ cup water
½ finely chopped green bell pepper
1 cup ketchup
8 hamburger buns

Prepare ahead: Chop the onion and the bell pepper and place them into a small re-closeable bag and seal. In a seperate bag mix the ketchup, mustard, vinegar, sugar, salt, chili powder, pepper and water and seal the bag.
At camp: Using the open foil method crumble the ground beef onto a piece of prepared foil. Add the chopped onion and the chopped bell pepper. Lie the foil with the ingredients onto the hot coals and cook until peppers and onions are tender stirring occasionally for about 7 to 10 minutes. Carefully stir in prepared sauce and heat through. Serve on buns.
Serves 4

Gumbo Burgers

1 pound ground beef
1-10 ounce can condensed
1 Tablespoon Worcestershire sauce
chicken gumbo soup
8 hamburger buns

At camp: Using the open foil method crumble ground beef onto a piece of prepared foil. Cook on hot coals stirring occasionally until done about 5 minutes. Open soup, carefully stir in Worcestershire sauce & add to ground beef. Heat through. Serve on buns.
Serves 4

Stuffed Pork Chops

4 pork chops cut 1" thick
½-7 ounce package seasoned
coating mix for pork
1¼ cups pork flavored stuffing mix
Cooking oil
½ cup water

At camp: Cut a pocket in each pork chop cutting to the bone in the largest area of the meat. In a large re-closeable bag add the ½ cup of water to the stuffing mix and toss to moisten the bread crumbs. Coat the pork chops on each side with the seasoned coating mix. Stuff each pork chop with ¼ of the stuffing mixture. Using the standard foil method place each stuffed pork chop on a piece of prepared foil. Wrap *do not pierce a hole in the foil.* Lie the pouches onto the hot coals and cook for 5 minutes. Turn pouches over and cook for another 5 minutes.
Serves 4

Sweet 'n Sour Ham Slices

4 ham steaks cut ½" thick
½ cup vinegar
1 Tablespoon molasses
¼ cup brown sugar
1 Tablespoon dry mustard
2 Tablespoons water
1½ cups orange juice

Prepare ahead: Combine all ingredients in a large re-closeable bag except the ham slices. Seal the bag.
At camp: Using the open foil method place the ham slices into the center of a piece of prepared foil. Pour the pre-mixed ingredients over the ham slices. Lie the foil with the ham and the premixed sauce onto the hot coals and cook for 5 minutes. Turn the ham slices over and cook for an additional 5 minutes or until the ham is done and the sauce is thickened.
Serves 4

Fire Roasted Pork Loin

1½ to 2 pounds boneless pork loin roast
¾ cup water
1-1 ounce envelope onion soup mix

At camp: Mix the water and the soup mix. Using the standard foil method place the roast on a large piece of prepared foil. Turn the edges of the foil up and pour soup mixture over the roast. Wrap but *do not pierce a hole in the foil*. Place the wrapped roast onto the hot coals and cook for 40 minutes, turning ¼ turn every 10 minutes. Remove from hot coals and let stand for 5 minutes.
Serves 4

Stuffed Tenderloin

1½ to 2 pounds boneless pork tenderloin roast
1-10 ounce cream of celery soup condensed
¾ cup water
1 teaspoon Worcestershire sauce
1¼ cups dry stuffing mix
¼ cup water
unseasoned meat tenderizer

Prepare ahead: Cut the roast through the middle not quite all the way through the meat. Open like a book and pound roast flat to about ½ to ¾ inch thick. Sprinkle with meat tenderizer. Combine the dry stuffing mix, ¼ cup water and ¼ cup condensed cream of celery soup. Spread the stuffing mixture evenly over the roast and roll the roast as tight as possible and secure with kitchen string. Place the rolled roast into a re-closeable bag and seal. In a separate re-closeable bag mix the remaining condensed soup, ¾ cup water and Worcestershire sauce and seal the bag.

At camp: Using the standard foil method place the rolled roast into a large piece of prepared foil and pour the soup mixture over the roast. Wrap but *do not pierce a hole in the foil* and place the wrapped roast onto the hot coals. Cook for 40 minutes, turning ¼ turn every 10 minutes. Remove from the hot coals and let rest for 5 minutes. Cut cross wise into 1" thick slices.
Serves 4

Glazed Pork Loin Steaks

1½ pounds boneless pork loin roast cut cross-wise into 1" slices
1 Tablespoon garlic powder
1 Tablespoon dry onion flakes
½ cup vinegar
3 Tablespoons honey
2 Tablespoons cooking oil
1 teaspoon dry mustard
salt and pepper
2 Tablespoons extra cooking oil

Prepare ahead: Combine the garlic powder, onion flakes, vinegar, honey, 2 Tablespoons oil and dry mustard in a small re-closeable bag and seal.
At camp: Using the open foil method pour the extra 2 Tablespoons of oil onto each of four pieces of prepared foil and place each pork steak in the center of the foil. Lie onto the hot coals and cook turning once to brown each side of the pork steaks. Remove the pork steaks from the fire. Pour premixed glaze over the pork steaks and wrap using the standard foil method. Lie the pouches onto the hot coals and cook for 8 minutes or until no longer pink.
Serves 4

Barbequed Smoked Sausage

1-12 ounce smoked sausage
1-12 ounce bottle barbeque sauce

At camp: Slice the sausage diagonally into ½" slices. Using the open foil method place the sliced sausage onto a piece of prepared foil and pour the barbeque sauce over the sausage and stir to coat all pieces. Lie directly onto the hot coals and cook for approximately 15 minutes or until sauce is caramelized.
Serves 4

Shrimp in Garlic Butter

¼ cup margarine
2 teaspoons parsley flakes
16 ounces medium sized
pre-cooked shrimp
8 ounces small whole mushrooms (or 1-4ounce can)

2 teaspoons garlic powder
1 teaspoon paprika
1 green bell pepper
½ teaspoon salt

Prepare ahead: Melt the margarine and stir in the parsley, garlic powder, and paprika. Cool and place the mixed margarine into a re-closeable bag and seal.
At camp: Using the standard foil method place all of the shrimp into the center of a large piece of prepared foil. Cut the bell pepper into bite size pieces, wash the mushrooms and add the peppers and whole mushrooms to the shrimp. Open the bag of seasoned margarine and squeeze the contents into center of the shrimp and vegetables. Wrap but *do not pierce a hole in the foil.* Lie onto the hot coals and cook for 3 minutes. Shake the foil pouch to mix up the ingredients and cook for another 5 minutes or until the peppers are tender.
Serves 4

Shrimp 'n Sauce

1½ pounds medium size pre cooked shrimp
1-15 ounce jar marinara sauce
1-4 ounce can mushrooms drained
Parmesan cheese

At camp: Using the standard foil method place all of the shrimp into the center of a large piece of prepared foil. Add the marinara sauce and mushrooms stirring to coat the shrimp and mushrooms. Wrap and place the pouch onto the hot coals and cook for 10 to 15 minutes or until heated through.
Serves 4

Poached Salmon Fillets

4-4 ounce pieces of salmon fillets
1 teaspoon onion powder
1 teaspoon parsley flakes
Water

2 Tablespoons margarine
1 teaspoon garlic powder
1 teaspoon seasoned salt
½ teaspoon paprika

Prepare ahead: Spread the margarine on one side of each salmon fillet. Sprinkle the seasonings onto the buttered side of each salmon fillet and place each fillet into a separate re-closeable bag and seal.
At camp: Using the standard foil method place each salmon fillet buttered side up into the center of a piece of prepared foil. Pour about ¼ cup water into each package being careful not to wash the seasonings off of the fillets. Wrap but *do not pierce a hole in the foil.* Lie the pouches onto the hot coals and cook for 8 minutes or until salmon is flaky.
Serves 4

Halibut and Vegetables

4-4 ounce halibut fillets
1 teaspoon seasoned salt
½ teaspoon pepper
½ teaspoon paprika
2 carrots
1 teaspoon parsley flakes
3 stalks celery
1 cup water
4 green onions (optional)
3 Tablespoons lemon juice

Prepare ahead: Shred the carrots and the celery. Finely chop the green onions and place them into a re-sealable bag with the carrots and the celery. Pour 2 Tablespoons lemon juice into the bag with the vegetables and shake the bag to coat the vegetables and seal the bag. **At camp:** Using the open foil method place all of the halibut fillets into the center of a single piece of prepared foil and sprinkle each fillet with the paprika, seasoned salt, parsley, 1 Tablespoon lemon juice and pepper. Pour the water into the vegetables. Pour the vegetable mixture with the water over the fillets. Lie onto the hot coals and cook for 5 to 10 minutes or until fillets are flaky.
Serves 4

Cod Fillets with Lime Sauce

4-4 ounce cod fillets
¾ cup vegetable oil
1/3 cup lime juice
1 teaspoon paprika
1 Tablespoon corn starch
½ teaspoon sugar

Prepare ahead: Place the cod fillets into a gallon size re-closeable bag. Add the oil, lime juice, sugar and paprika. Seal the bag and shake it gently to mix the sauce and to coat the cod fillets.
At camp: Using the standard foil method place each cod fillet onto a piece of prepared foil. Add the corn starch to the lime sauce mixture. Reclose the bag and shake it to mix the ingredients. Pour the lime sauce over the fillets. Wrap and lie the pouches onto the hot coals and cook for 15 minutes or until the fillets are tender and flaky.
Serves 4

Seasoned Potato Wedges

4 or 5 small red or russet potatoes
Choice of seasoning combinations listed below

Prepare ahead: Scrub the potatoes. In a medium size re-closeable bag add the seasonings to the oil and seal the bag.
At camp: Cut the potatoes lengthwise into 8 or 10 wedges per potato. Put the potatoes in the bag with the oil and seasonings. Close the bag and shake it to coat the potatoes. Using the standard foil method place the oil coated potatoes into the center of a piece of prepared foil. Wrap and lie the pouches onto the hot coals and cook for 10 minutes. Open the foil and turn the potatoes over and cook uncovered for another 10 to 20 minutes or until golden brown and tender.
Serves 4

Italian
3 Tablespoons cooking oil
1 Tablespoon Italian seasoning
1 teaspoon garlic powder

Cajun
3 Tablespoons cooking oil
2 Tablespoons Creole seasoning
¼ teaspoon cayenne pepper

Basic
3 Tablespoons cooking oil
1 Tablespoon seasoned salt
1 teaspoon paprika
1 Tablespoon parsley flakes

Ranch
3 Tablespoons cooking oil
2 Tablespoons dry ranch dressing mix

Southwestern
3 Tablespoons cooking oil
1 Tablespoon cumin
1 teaspoon garlic powder
¼ teaspoon cayenne
1 teaspoon parsley flakes
½ teaspoon onion powder

Parmesan

1 teaspoon parsley flakes
2 Tablespoons dry parmesan cheese
½ teaspoon onion powder
1 Tablespoon rosemary

Garlic and Rosemary

1 teaspoon parsley flakes
3 Tablespoons cooking oil
1 Tablespoon rosemary
1 Tablespoon garlic powder
3 Tablespoons cooking oil

Baked Potato

4 large baking potatoes
margarine or butter
sour cream

Prepare ahead: Scrub the potatoes.
At camp: Cut a slit lengthwise into each potato approximately 2"
long. Roll each potato in a piece of foil large enough to overlap the
potato at least 2". Twist both ends of the foil and lie the wrapped
potatoes onto the hot coals. Cook for 1 hour turning ¼ of a turn every
15 minutes. Open the potatoes and add margarine and sour cream if
desired.
*Variations: Stuff potatoes with cheese and broccoli page 97, or
stroganoff page 96 or with taco fillings page 98.*
Serves 4

Fire Roasted Vegetables

½ pound baby red potatoes
1 green bell pepper
1½ cups fresh broccoli
½ cup baby carrots
florets
½ cup cooking oil
1 Tablespoon garlic powder
1 teaspoon salt
½ teaspoon pepper
1 Tablespoon parsley flakes
1 Tablespoon onion powder

Prepare ahead: Wash the potatoes and the broccoli. In a re-closeable bag combine the oil, garlic powder, pepper, salt, onion powder, and parsley flakes and seal the bag.
At camp: Cut the potatoes in half and cut the pepper and the broccoli into bite sized pieces. Using the standard foil method place all of the vegetables into the center of a large piece of prepared foil. Pour the seasoned oil mixture over the vegetables. Wrap and lie the pouch onto the hot coals and cook for 20 minutes or until vegetables are tender.
* Variation: 1 package of dry ranch dressing mix can be mixed in the oil in place of the seasonings.
Serves 4

Fire Roasted Corn on the Cob

4 ears corn on the cob in husks
24 paper towels still connected together

Prepare ahead: Without removing the husks pull down on the corn husk to expose the silk leaving the husks attached to the stem end. Remove the silk and re-wrap the corn in the husks and place them into a gallon sized re-closeable bag and seal.

At camp: Pull the corn husks back down to the stem on each of the corn cobs without removing the husks. Cut through the cob to release it from the stem end but do not remove the cob from the husks and stem. Pull the husks back up around the cob. Wrap each corn on the cob in the husks with strips of six paper towels around corn in the husks being careful to cover the ends of the corn on the cob. Dip each wrapped corn on the cob into water that is in a gallon sized bag to saturate the paper towels and lie each corn on the cob onto a piece of prepared foil. Wrap like a baked potato. Lie each corn on the cob onto the hot coals and cook for 1 hour turning ¼ turn every 15 minutes. Unwrap and remove the corn from the foil and the husks being careful of the hot steam. Butter and serve.
Serves 4

Poached Eggs

8 eggs
salt and pepper

At camp: Using the open foil method prepare four pieces of foil folding each side up 3" to 4". Pour 1 cup of water into each piece of prepared foil. Place two opened eggs in each foil. Salt and pepper to taste. Cover with an extra piece of foil and lie the pouches onto the hot coals. Cook for 10 minutes checking occasionally until done as desired.
Serves 4

Bacon or Sausage

Bacon or sausage links, or patties

Place bacon strips or sausage onto a piece of prepared open foil. Lie the foil and meat onto the hot coals and cook turning once until well done.

Chocolate Orange Cake

6 large oranges
1-9 ounce chocolate cake mix
1 egg
¼ cup water
whipped topping
6 teaspoons sugar

Prepare ahead: Mix the egg and the milk in a small re-closeable bag and seal.

At camp: Cut top off of each orange about 1" from the top leaving it hinged if possible. Scoop out the inside of the oranges leaving about ½" of orange pulp in the sides of the peel. Drain excess juice from the oranges and sprinkle the inside of each orange peel with 1 teaspoon of sugar. Add the cake mix to the bag of liquid ingredients and shake the closed bag to mix it thoroughly. Pour the cake mix into the oranges filling each one about 2/3 full. Close the hinged lid on each orange. Using the standard foil method place each orange *upright* onto a piece of prepared foil. Wrap and place all of the wrapped cakes upright into a foil pan and place the foil pan with the oranges directly onto the hot coals. *Do not allow oranges to roll over* and cook uncovered for 30 to 35 minutes. Remove them from the fire. Unwrap each orange and let set for 5 minutes. Open the hinged lids and top with whipped topping.

Makes 6

Tip: placing the wrapped cake filled oranges in a foil muffin tin helps to keep them from rolling over and spilling the cake batter during cooking.

Chapter Four
Clothes Hanger Cooking

Make your own disposable griddle! A quick method that can be used directly on the hot coals or on a rack over the keyhole fire pit. This method is great for breakfast because you don't have to wait as long to build up the hot coals.

Link Sausage page 60, Campfire Toast page 60
and Fried Egg page 61

Campfire Toast

Butter both sides of the bread slices and place them onto a prepared clothes hanger pan. Lie the pan with the buttered bread directly onto the hot coals and cook until golden brown turning once to brown both sides.
* *Tip:* Toasting bread products on the rack over a keyhole fire pit can result in dry bread if the fire is not hot enough under the pan. I recommend placing them directly onto the hot coals.

Bacon or Sausage

Sausage (link or patty) or sliced bacon

Place the meat onto a prepared clothes hanger pan and cook directly on the hot coals until browned on all sides and done in the middle turning as needed.

Fried Eggs

8 eggs
cooking oil
salt and pepper

Prepare ahead: Crack open the eggs and put them into a re-closeable bag and seal. Place the bag of eggs into a container with a lid and close the lid and pack.

At camp: Prepare two wire clothes hangers. Pour about 2 Tablespoons of oil onto each pan and place them onto a rack over the keyhole fire pit. * Heat the oil until it sizzles when a drop of water is dropped on it. Open the bag of eggs and pour out one at a time (about 4 eggs per pan). Cook until done turning carefully to avoid tearing the foil. Salt and pepper to taste.

* The rack needs to be very level to prevent the eggs and the oil from sliding off of the pan and into the fire.

Serves 4

Hash Browns

2 cups dehydrated hash browns
salt and pepper
½ cup margarine

Prepare ahead: Place the dehydrated hash browns into a gallon re-closeable bag and seal the bag.
At camp: The night before: Open the bag of hash browns and pour enough water into the bag to a level that is about 2" above the hash browns and re-seal the bag. Let them set in the bag of water over night.
In the morning: Prepare two clothes hanger pans and place them directly onto the hot coals. Place 2 Tablespoons of margarine onto each pan and heat until it melts. Open the bag of hash browns slightly and drain out any excess water squeezing the bag gently to remove as much water as possible. Finish opening the bag and pour half of the hash browns out onto each prepared pan with the melted margarine. Cook turning carefully to avoid tearing the foil as needed adding more margarine when turning the hash browns. Salt and pepper to taste.
Serves 4

Apple Cinnamon Pancakes

2 cups buttermilk pancake mix
1 Tablespoon cinnamon
1 teaspoon vanilla
½ cup water
1½ cups applesauce

Prepare ahead: Place the pancake mix and the cinnamon into a gallon size re-closeable bag and seal.
At camp: Prepare two clothes hanger pans. Open the bag of pancake mix. Stir in the apple sauce, vanilla and water. Place the pans on a rack over the keyhole fire. Pour the pancakes onto the pans using approximately ¼ cup mix per pancake. Cook until the edges of the pancakes are dry and bubbles appear on the tops. Turn and continue cooking until the bottom of the pancakes are browned. Serve with butter and maple syrup.
Makes 8 - 6" pancakes

Buttermilk Pancakes

2 cups buttermilk pancake mix
1½ cups water
1 Tablespoon vanilla

At camp: In large re-closeable bag combine the pancake mix, water and vanilla. Close the bag and shake it well to mix it thoroughly. Using two prepared foil pans that are set on a rack over the keyhole fire pour the pancake batter onto each pan using approximately ¼ cup batter for each pancake. Cook turning when the edges of the pancakes turn dry and bubbles appear on the tops. Turn over and continue cooking until the pancakes are golden brown on both sides. **Makes 8 - 6" pancakes**

Cranberry Orange Pancakes

2 cups buttermilk pancake mix
½ cup water
½ cup jellied cranberry sauce cut into ½" pieces
1 cup orange juice
2 Tablespoons sugar

Prepare ahead: Place the pancake mix into a gallon sized re-
closeable bag and seal. Cut the ½ cup jellied cranberry sauce into ½"
chunks and put into a separate smaller re-closeable bag and seal.
At camp: Prepare two clothes hanger pans. Open the bag of the
pancake mix and stir in the water, sugar and orange juice. Add the ½
cup cranberry sauce and fold in gently to leave small lumps of the
cranberry sauce in the batter. Place the prepared clothes hanger pans
onto a rack over the keyhole fire pit and pour approximately ¼ cup
batter onto the pans for each pancake. Cook until the edges of the
pancakes are dry and bubbles form on the tops. Turn and continue to
cook until bottom is browned.
Makes 8 - 6" pancakes

French Toast

8 slices Texas Toast style bread
7 eggs
2 Tablespoons milk
¼ teaspoon salt
1/8 teaspoon pepper
margarine

Prepare ahead: Break the eggs open into a gallon sized re-closeable bag and add the milk, salt and pepper. Close the bag and shake it to mix the ingredients.
At camp: Prepare a clothes hanger pan and place it onto a rack over the keyhole fire pit and put 2 Tablespoons of margarine on the pan to melt. Open the bag of egg mixture and dip each piece of bread into the egg mixture quickly to avoid the bread from getting so soggy that it falls apart. Immediately place each coated slice of bread on the heated pan and cook turning once until browned on each side.
Serves 4

Campfire Triple Decker

12 slices prepared French toast (recipe above)
8 slices turkey lunch meat
4 slices American cheese
8 slices ham lunch meat
4 slices mozzarella cheese

At camp: Layer sandwiches in order given:1 slice of prepared French toast (recipe above), 2 slices of ham, 1 slice of mozzarella cheese, 1 slice of prepared French toast, 2 slices of turkey, 1 slice of American cheese and 1 slice of prepared French toast. Place each sandwich on a prepared clothes hanger pan on a rack over the keyhole fire pit and cover with apiece of foil. Grill the sandwiches turning once until the cheese melts.
Serves 4

French BLT

8 slices prepared French toast (Recipe above)
8 slices bacon
8 slices tomato
8 lettuce leaves

At Camp: Prepare a clothes hanger pan. Cook the bacon on the foil pan until it is crispy. Drain the bacon on a layer of paper towels. Assemble the bacon, lettuce and tomato between two slices prepared French toast and serve.
Serves 4

Toasted Garlic Bread

4 slices French bread 2" thick
Margarine
Garlic powder
Paprika
Parsley flakes

At camp: Spread the margarine onto both sides of each slice of French bread and sparingly sprinkle both sides of the buttered bread with the paprika, garlic powder and parsley flakes. Place each prepared slice of bread onto a foil pan and set it directly onto the hot coals and cook turning once until golden brown on each side.
Serves 4

Sizzlin' Steak

Four 6 to 8 oz steaks cut 1" thick
Unseasoned meat tenderizer
Garlic salt

Prepare ahead: Sprinkle each side of all of the steaks with the meat tenderizer and the garlic salt. Place each seasoned steak into a recloseable bag and seal.

At camp: Prepare two clothes hanger pans. Lie the pans directly onto the hot coals. Place two steaks on each pan. Cook according to the chart below as desired turning once half way through the total cooking time. Remove them from the heat, cover and let rest for 5 minutes.

* Steaks continue to cook for a few minutes after removing them from the heat.

Serves 4

Rare: 4 to 5 minutes per side
Medium: 6 to 7 minutes per side
Well Done: 9 to 10 minutes per side

Smothered Chops

4 Pork chops cut ½" thick
1 Tablespoon Worcestershire sauce
1-10 ounce can condensed cream of mushroom soup
½ cup water

Prepare ahead: Combine the condensed soup, Worcestershire sauce and water in a re-closeable bag. Seal the bag and shake it to mix the ingredients.
At camp: Place the pork chops onto two prepared and preheated foil pans. Cook the Pork chops on a rack over the keyhole fire until done: for approximately 5 minutes on each side. Pour the premixed soup mixture over the pork chops lifting each pork chop to allow the sauce to flow under the meat. Cook for another 10 minutes or until the sauce is heated though.
Serves 4

Chili Chops

4 pork chops cut ½" thick
1 Tablespoon cumin
1 Tablespoon chili powder
1 teaspoon garlic powder
1 teaspoon onion powder
2 Tablespoons cooking oil
Salt and pepper
1 teaspoon dry mustard

Prepare ahead: Combine the chili powder, cumin, garlic powder, dry mustard and onion powder. Rub the mixture on both sides of each pork chop and place them into a re-closeable bag and seal the bag.
At camp: Place 1 Tablespoon of oil on each of two prepared foil pans. Place the pans on a rack over the keyhole fire. Heat the oil until it sizzles when a drop of water is dropped on it. Place the pork chops onto the preheated pans and cook for approximately 5 to 7 minutes per side or until the pork chops are browned and cooked through.
Serves 4

Pineapple Ham Steak

2 ham steaks cut in half
½ cup pineapple juice
½ cup brown sugar
2 Tablespoons corn starch
4 pineapple slices

Prepare ahead: In a re-closeable bag mix the pineapple juice, brown sugar and corn starch and seal the bag.

At camp: On each of the two prepared foil pans place two of the pineapple slices with a ham steak placed on the top of each pineapple slice. Pour the premixed glaze mixture over each of the ham steaks lifting the steaks to allow the glaze mixture to run underneath. Cook on a rack over the keyhole fire pit for approximately 10 minutes. Turn bringing the pineapple slices to the top with each ham steak. Cook for another 10 minutes or until glaze is set and ham is cooked through.

Serves 4

Honey Glazed Chicken Tenders

1½ lbs breaded chicken tenders
1 teaspoon salt
½ cup cooking oil
¼ cup brown sugar
¼ cup honey
2 Tablespoons lemon juice
1 teaspoon paprika
1 teaspoon parsley flakes
1 green bell pepper cut into ½" strips
½ red onion sliced and separated into rings

Prepare ahead: Combine ¼ cup of the cooking oil with the salt, brown sugar, honey, lemon juice, paprika and parsley into a re-closeable bag and seal the bag.
At camp: Divide the remaining ¼ cup of the cooking oil onto two prepared foil pans. Place the pans on a rack over the keyhole fire. Heat the oil until it sizzles when a drop of water is dropped on it. Divide the onion rings, bell pepper strips and chicken tenders equally onto the two pans and cook until the vegetables are crisp tender stirring occasionally. Pour the sauce over the chicken with the vegetables and stir to coat them evenly. Cook turning often until sauce caramelizes: about 10 to 15 minutes.
Serves 4

Malibu Chicken

4 precooked and breaded chicken breast patties
hamburger buns (optional)
4 thin slices ham
4 slices Swiss cheese

At camp: Place the chicken breasts onto a prepared foil pan on a rack over the keyhole fire. Cook until the chicken breast patties are browned on both sides and heated through. Place a slice of ham on each chicken patty and top with a slice of Swiss cheese. Cover the topped patties loosely with a piece of foil that has been sprayed with a non-stick cooking spray placing the sprayed side down and cook approximately 10 more minutes or until cheese is melted. Serve as is or on a bun.
Serves 4

Chapter Five
Double Pan Cooking

Taco Tater page 98

Potato Pie

1 ½ cups dehydrated hash browns
3 Tablespoons chopped onion
3 Tablespoons dehydrated chopped garlic
½ pound sausage
6 eggs
2 cups shredded cheddar cheese
¼ cup milk
¼ teaspoon salt
1/8 teaspoon pepper

Prepare ahead: Place the dehydrated hash browns into a gallon sized re-closeable bag and seal the bag. Break the eggs open into a smaller re-closeable bag and add milk, salt and pepper. Stir the egg mixture and seal the bag. Place the bag of egg mixture into a container and close the lid.

At camp: *The night before:* Open the hash browns and pour enough water into the bag to bring the water level 2" above the hash browns and seal the bag. *The next morning:* Partially open the soaked hash browns and drain off the excess water squeezing gently to remove as much water as possible. Place two prepared foil cake pans on a rack over the keyhole fire pit. Crumble half of the sausage into each pan. When the sausage starts to sizzle add half of the drained potatoes into each pan and sprinkle the potatoes and sausage in each pan with half of the seasonings. Turn when the bottom of the hash browns become golden brown. Cook for another 5 minutes. Add half of the egg mixture into each pan. Stir occasionally until eggs are almost set. Top the ingredients in each pan with half of the shredded cheddar cheese and cover each pan with a piece of foil. Cook until the cheese is melted. Cut the ingredients in each pan in half for each serving.
Serves 4

Italian Omelet

6 eggs
¼ cup milk
¼ teaspoon salt
1/8 teaspoon pepper
16 ounces frozen Italian vegetables
½ ounce sliced pepperoni
1½ cups shredded mozzarella cheese
¼ cup margarine

Prepare ahead: In a medium sized re-closeable bag mix the eggs, milk, salt and pepper and seal the bag. Place the frozen vegetables into a second re-closeable bag and seal the bag.

At camp: Place two prepared foil cake pans on a rack over the keyhole fire pit. Melt half of the margarine in each pan. When the margarine is melted place half of the thawed vegetables and half of the pepperoni slices into each pan. Pour half of the egg mixture over the vegetables and sliced pepperoni in each pan. Cook lifting the edges of the eggs occasionally to allow the ucooked portion to run underneath the cooked portion until the eggs are almost set. Carefully fold the omelet in half. Top each omelet with half of the cheese. Cover each pan tightly with a piece of foil and cook until the cheese is melted. Cut each omelet in half for each serving.

Serves 4

Ham and Cheese Omelet

8 eggs
1½ cups diced ham
2 Tablespoons margarine
¼ cup milk
¼ teaspoon salt
1/8 teaspoon pepper
1½ cups shredded cheddar cheese
¼ cup margarine

Prepare ahead: In a re-closeable bag mix the eggs, milk, salt and pepper and seal the bag.

At Camp: Place two prepared foil cake pans on a rack over the keyhole fire pit and melt 1 Tablespoon of the margarine in each pan. Pour half of the egg mixture over the melted margarine in each pan. Cook carefully lifting the edges of the eggs to allow the uncooked portions to run underneath the cooked portions until the eggs are almost set. Place half of the cubed ham in a line down the center of the eggs in each pan. Sprinkle each omelet with ½ cup of the cheese. Fold the omelets over into thirds enveloping the ham and the cheese in the center of the eggs. Top each omelet with ¼ cup cheese. Cover tightly with a piece of foil and cook until the cheese melts. Cut each omelet in half for each serving.

Serves 4

Breakfast Burrito

6 eggs
½ pound bulk pork sausage
2 cups shredded cheddar cheese
8-12" flour tortillas
2 Tablespoon milk
1/8 teaspoon pepper
½ teaspoon salt

Prepare ahead: In a gallon sized plastic re-closeable bag mix the eggs, milk, salt, pepper and seal the bag.
At camp: Prepare two foil pans and place them onto a rack over the keyhole fire pit. Brown and crumble half of the sausage into each of the two pans. Drain off the fat from the sausage and add the prepared egg mixture stirring as they cook. When the eggs are almost set sprinkle half of the cheese on top of the ingredients in each pan and cover them with foil. Cook for approximately 5 more minutes or until the cheese melts. Serve on tortillas and pass the hot sauce.
Serves 4

Canned Biscuits

1 can biscuits of any variety

At camp: Open the can of biscuits and arrange them into one prepared foil cake pan. Place a second pan on the top upside down for a lid and secure. Place the pan on a rack over the keyhole fire pit and put a small scoop of hot coals on the top pan for an even temperature. Cook for 10 minutes or until golden brown.
Serves 4

Buttermilk Biscuits

2¼ cups flour
½ teaspoon salt
4 teaspoons baking powder
1/3 cup shortening
¾ cup buttermilk

Prepare ahead: In a gallon sized plastic bag mix the flour, salt and baking powder. Being careful not to tear the bag cut in the shortening with a fork until it is the size of peas (The ingredients can be mixed in a bowl and transferred to the bag if desired.) and seal the bag. Place the buttermilk into a smaller re-closeable bag and seal.

At camp: Open the large bag and pour in the buttermilk. Re-seal the bag squeezing out all of the air. Mix the ingredients in the closed bag by kneading with your hands until it is mixed thoroughly. Flatten the dough in the bag with your hands so that it is about half the size of the bag and about 1½" thick. Open the bag and cut down both side seams of the bag. Cut the dough into 9 pieces. Roll each piece of dough into a ball. Arrange the dough balls evenly spaced one in the center and eight around the edge of one prepared foil cake pan. Put the second pan on the top upside down and secure. Place on a rack over the keyhole fire pit and bake for 5 minutes. Turn both pans over together with the biscuits and bake another 5 to 10 minutes or until biscuits are golden brown and flaky inside.

* If the heat under the rack is not hot enough a small scoop of hot coals can be added to the top pan to speed the cooking time.
Makes 9

Hash and Egg Cups

1-15 ounce can corned beef hash
6 eggs
salt and pepper
6 slices American cheese
one foil muffin tin

Prepare ahead: Break open the eggs into a small re-closeable bag and seal the bag. Place the bag of eggs into a container with a lid and close the lid.
At camp: Spray the foil muffin tin with a non-stick cooking spray. Press 2 to 3 Tablespoons of the corned beef hash into each muffin cup pressing up the sides as well as the bottom forming a cup. Place one slice of cheese in each cup forming it to fit the hash cup as closely as possible. Pour eggs out one at a time placing one in each hash cup. Salt and pepper to taste. Cover with a piece of foil and place directly into the hot coals. Cook for 15 to 20 minutes or until the eggs are set.
Makes 6

French Toast Pie

5 eggs
½ cup milk
1 teaspoon vanilla
¼ teaspoon salt
4 teaspoons margarine
2/3 cup flour
1 teaspoons maple flavoring

Prepare ahead: In a large re-closeable bag mix the eggs, milk, vanilla and salt. Seal the bag. Place the pre-measured flour in a second bag and seal.

At camp: Prepare two foil cake pans. In the large bag add the flour to the egg mixture and seal the bag. Shake the bag to mix the ingredients. Melt the margarine in one pan placed on a rack over the keyhole fire. Pour the mixed ingredients into the pan with the melted butter. Cover the pan with a second pan turned upside down and secure. Cook for 15 to 17 minutes or until a knife inserted into the center comes out clean. (This will fall when you take the lid off) Serve with maple syrup.

Serves 4

Muffins

1-8 ounce package muffin mix any variety
1 egg
¼ cup milk

Prepare ahead: Mix egg and milk in a large re-closeable bag and seal the bag.

At camp: Prepare one foil cake pan. Add the muffin mix to the milk and egg mixture in the re-closeable bag. Seal and shake the bag to mix the ingredients. Pour into the prepared pan and cover with a second pan turned upside down and secure the pans together. Place the pan with the muffin mix on a rack over the keyhole fire. Put a small scoop of hot coals on the top pan to create an even tempurature. Cook for 10 to 12 minutes or until muffins are done in the center. Cut the muffins into wedges to serve.

Tip: One 7 ounce corn bread or cake mix can be prepared the same way as muffins.

Serves 4

Sausage Gravy

1 pound bulk pork breakfast sausage
4 cups milk
¾ cup flour
salt and pepper

At camp: Divide the sausage between two prepared foil cake pans and place the pans on a rack over the keyhole fire pit. Brown and crumble the sausage stirring it often. Remove the sausage with a slotted spoon to a plate and set it aside. If there is not at least three Tablespoons of drippings in each pan from the sausage add margarine to make approximately three Tablespoons and heat until it melts. Stir 6 Tablespoons of flour into each pan. Pour 2 cups of the milk into each pan and stir with a wire whip until the mixture is smooth. Heat the gravy stirring it often until it is thickened and bubbly. Return the sausage to the pans and stir. Season to taste with salt and pepper. Serve over biscuits or toast or hash browns or baked potatoes.
Serves 4

Chicken Pot Pie

2 cups diced cooked chicken
1 cup frozen mixed vegetables
2-10 ounce cans chicken gravy
½ cup milk
1 cup biscuit mix
1 egg

Prepare ahead: Place the biscuit mix into a re-closeable gallon sized bag and seal the bag. In a separate re-closeable bag mix the milk with the egg and seal the bag. Place the vegetables into a third bag and seal.

At Camp: Prepare two foil cake pans. Add the milk mixture to the biscuit mix in the gallon bag. Close the bag squeezing out the air and mix well by kneading it with your hands. Leaving the mixed dough in the bag place it into one of the pans pressing it down into the pan until it fits the pan. Remove the dough from the pan and the bag keeping it in the shape of the pan and spray the pan with a non-stick cooking spray. Put the dough back into the pan and cover it with a second pan turned upside down and secure. Place the pan on a rack over the keyhole fire pit and cook for 10 minutes or until dough is lightly browned on the bottom. Remove the partially cooked dough from the pan and set aside. Mix the chicken, gravy and thawed vegetables together in a re-closeable bag and pour the mixture into the empty pan. Place the cooked dough on the top of the chicken filling mixture with the browned side of the dough facing up. Cover it with a second pan turned upside down and secure. Replace the pan on a rack over the keyhole fire pit and cook for approximately 20 minutes or until the gravy mixture is bubbly and dough is cooked through.

Serves 4

Chicken and Stuffing Dumplings

1-10 ounce can chicken drained
1-10 ounce can cream of
1 cup frozen mixed vegetables
chicken soup
1 cup milk divided
1 cup biscuit mix
1½ teaspoons poultry seasoning
1 teaspoon sage

Prepare ahead: Mix the dry biscuit mix, poultry seasoning and sage in a large re-closeable bag and seal the bag. Pour ½ cup of the milk *each into two separate bags* and seal the bags. Place the vegetables into a third bag and seal.

At camp: In a prepared foil cake pan mix the drained chicken, condensed soup, ½ cup of the milk and thawed vegetables. In the large re-closeable bag stir together biscuit mixture and ½ cup of the milk in a gallon bag and drop the dumpling dough by heaping Tablespoonfuls onto chicken mixture in the pan. Cover the pan with a second pan turned upside down and secure. Place the pan on a rack over the keyhole fire pit and add a small scoop of hot coals to the top of the second pan to create an even temperature. Cook for 15 to 20 minutes or until the dumplings are set but not browned and chicken mixture is bubbly.

Serves 4

Chicken ala King

2-6 ounce cans chicken
1-10 ounce can cream of mushroom soup
1-4 ounce can mushrooms
¾ cup milk
1 teaspoon parsley
½ teaspoon Worcestershire sauce
1 can buttermilk biscuits

At camp: Prepare three foil cake pans. Open the canned biscuits and arrange them into one pan in a single layer and cover them with a second pan turned upside down and secure. Drain the mushrooms. Pour the mushrooms into the third foil pan and stir in the chicken, condensed soup, Worcestershire sauce, milk, and parsley. Place the chicken mixture on a rack over the keyhole fire *uncovered* and cook stirring often until the mixture is hot and bubbly. Meanwhile place prepared biscuits in the pan on a rack over the keyhole fire adding a small scoop of hot coals onto the top pan to create an even temperature and cook for approximately 15 minutes or until lightly browned.
To serve pour chicken mixture over cooked bisciuts.
Serves 4

Southwest Chicken Lasagna

3 cups diced cooked chicken
1 Tablespoon cumin
1 Tablespoon Worcestershire sauce
½-10 ounce soup can milk
2-3 ounce cans chopped green chiles
1-10 ounce can cream of chicken soup
1-10 ounce can cream of celery soup
1 Tablespoon garlic powder
10-8" flour tortillas
4 cups shredded cheddar cheese
salsa
sour cream

At camp: Prepare two foil cake pans. In a gallon sized plastic bag mix the chicken, condensed soups, milk, undrained chiles, onion powder, Worcestershire sauce, cumin and garlic powder. In each pan pour just enough of the chicken mixture to cover the bottom of the pans about ½" deep. Place a tortilla on the top of the mixture and pour more of the chicken mixture over the tortilla and sprinkle with a small amount of shredded cheddar cheese. Repeat the layers using 5 tortillas per pan ending with the sauce and cheese. Cover each pan with a second pan turned upside down adding a small scoop of hot coals on the top pan to create an even temperature. Place the pans on a rack over the keyhole fire pit and bake for 30 minutes or until the cheese is melted. Remove from heat and let stand for 5 minutes. Cut each pan into 4 wedges to serve. Top with salsa and sour cream if desired.
Serves 4

Citrus Chicken

1 pound precooked un-breaded chicken strips
1 Tablespoon dehydrated onion flakes
1/8 teaspoon pepper
8 ounces frozen sliced carrots
½ teaspoon salt
2/3 cup orange juice
1 Tablespoon cornstarch
1/3 cup orange marmalade
1 Tablespoon lemon juice
4 Tablespoons brown sugar
8 ounces frozen green beans
¼ cup honey

Prepare ahead: Place the orange juice, marmalade, lemon juice, brown sugar, honey, salt, pepper, onion flakes and corn starch in a large re-closeable bag. Shake the bag to mix the contents and seal.
At Camp: Prepare two foil cake pans. Divide the chicken, thawed green beans and thawed carrots into the two pans. Pour half of the premixed sauce into each pan. Cover each pan tightly with a piece of foil. Place the pans on a rack over the keyhole fire pit and cook for 10 to 15 minutes or until the ingredients are heated through and sauce has thickened.
Serves 4

Chili Pie

2-15 ounce cans chili
1-16 ounce pkg corn bread mix
1½ cups shredded cheddar cheese
2 eggs
2/3 cup milk

At camp: Prepare two foil cake pans. Pour one can of chili into each pan. Mix the corn bread in a large re-closeable bag with the milk and the egg. Pour half of the corn bread mixture over the chili in each pan. Cover each pan with a second pan turned upside down and secure. Place both pans on a rack over the keyhole fire pit adding a small scoop of hot coals on the top of each pan. Cook for 20 to 25 minutes or until the corn bread is done. Uncover the pans and sprinkle each with ¾ cup of the shredded cheese. Recover both pans and cook for 5 to 10 minutes or until cheese melts and the corn bread is done in the center.
Serves 4

Stew and Dumplings

2-15 ounce cans beef stew
¾ cup milk
1 cup biscuit mix

At camp: Prepare two foil cake pans. Pour one can of stew into each pan. Place the pans on a rack over the keyhole fire pit and heat the stew through until bubbly stirring occasionally. Combine the biscuit mix and the milk in a large re-closeable bag seal the bag and mix well. Drop the dumpling dough one at a time by heaping Tablespoons full onto the bubbling stew in both pans. Cover each pan with a second pan turned upside down and secure. Add a small scoop of hot coals on top of each of the second pans and cook 10 to 15 minutes or until dumplings are done.
Serves 4

Cheddar Burger Bake

1-10 ounce can condensed cream of mushroom soup
1 pound ground beef
¼ cup finely chopped onion
2-16 ounce cans sliced potatoes
1 cup shredded cheddar cheese
1-10 ounce can cheddar cheese soup
1-4 ounce can sliced mushrooms
¼ cup water
1 Tablespoon Worcestershire sauce

At camp: Prepare one foil cake pan. Brown and crumble the ground beef and onion in the pan placed on a rack over the keyhole fire pit and drain. Stir in the condensed soups, drained mushrooms, water, Worcestershire sauce, and drained potatoes. Top with the shredded cheese. Cover the pan with a second pan turned upside down and cook for 20 minutes or until the cheese is bubbly.
Serves 4

Tamale Pie

1 pound ground beef
1-16 ounce can tomato sauce
½ cup chopped olives
¼ teaspoon garlic powder
1 Tablespoon sugar
1 teaspoon salt
3 teaspoons chili powder
1½ cups shredded cheddar cheese
1 teaspoon cumin
¼ cup milk
1-8 ounce package corn muffin mix
1 egg

At camp: Prepare one foil pan and place the pan on a rack over the keyhole fire pit. Brown and crumble the ground beef and drain. Stir in the tomato sauce, olives, garlic powder, salt, sugar, and cumin. Mix the corn muffin mix with milk and egg in a large plastic bag and pour over the seasoned meat mixture. Cover the pan with a second pan turned upside down and secure. Add a small scoop of hot coals on the top pan to create an even temperature and cook for 20 minutes or until the corn bread is done. Remove the top pan and cover the contents with the shredded cheddar cheese. Recover the pan and secure. Cook for another 10 minutes or until the cheese is melted.
Serves 4

Campfire Pie

1 pound ground beef
1-10 ounce can condensed tomato soup
1-15 ounce can green beans
1-4 ounce package instant mashed potatoes
1½ cups shredded cheddar cheese
1 cup water
1 teaspoon salt
¼ teaspoon pepper
1 teaspoon beef bullion

At camp: In a medium sized re-closeable bag mix the instant mashed potatoes with the water. While the potatoes are setting up crumble the ground beef into one prepared foil pan and place the pan on a rack over the keyhole fire pit. Brown stirring occasionally and drain. Remove the pan from the heat. Stir in the drained green beans, tomato soup, bullion, salt and pepper and mix well. Spread the mashed potatoes over the meat mixture. Top the potatoes with the shredded cheddar cheese. Cover the pan with a second pan turned upside down and secure. Place the pan on a rack over the keyhole fire pit adding a small scoop of hot coals on the top pan to create an even temperature and cook for approximately 15 minutes or until meat mixture is bubbly and the cheese is melted.
Serves 4

Stroganoff Stuffed Potatoes

4 baker potatoes
1 pound ground beef
2-10 ounce cans beef gravy
½ cup sour cream
1-4 ounce can mushrooms
1 teaspoon beef bullion

At camp: Prepare the bake potatoes as instructed in recipe page 53. Fifteen minutes before the potatoes are done prepare one foil cake pan and place it on a rack over the keyhole fire pit. Brown and crumble the ground beef in the pan and drain. Stir in the gravy, bullion, drained mushrooms and sour cream. Heat through. Serve over baked potatoes. Top with additional sour cream if desired.
Serves 4

Cheddar Broccoli Stuffed Potatoes

4 baker potatoes
1-15 ounce jar cheddar cheese sauce
1-10 ounce pkg frozen chopped broccoli

At camp: Prepare the bake potatoes as instructed on page 53. Fifteen minutes before the potatoes are done prepare one foil cake pan. Add the thawed broccoli to the pan and enough water to just cover the broccoli. Place on a rack over the keyhole fire pit and cook for 5 to 10 minutes or until the broccoli is tender. *Do not let it boil dry.* Drain any liquid off from the broccoli and stir in the cheese sauce. Heat through. Serve on baked potatoes. Top with sour cream if desired.
Tip: Cooked crumbled bacon pieces can be substituted for the broccoli. Just add into the cheese sauce and heat through.
Serves 4

Taco Taters

4 baker potatoes
1 pound ground beef
1-1½ ounce pkg taco seasoning
2 cups shredded cheddar cheese
2 cups shredded lettuce
2 tomatoes chopped
1/3 cup water
sour cream
taco sauce

At camp: Prepare and bake potatoes as instructed on page 53. Fifteen minutes before potatoes are done prepare one foil cake pan. Place the foil pan on a rack over the keyhole fire pit. Brown and crumble ground beef in the pan and drain. Add the taco seasoning mix and water. Simmer stirring often until thickened. Serve over baked potatoes and top with shredded lettuce, shredded cheese and chopped tomatoes. Pass the taco sauce and sour cream.
Serves 4

Smokie Wraps

1-8 ounce package cocktail wieners
2 cans buttermilk biscuits
Prepared mustard
barbeque sauce

At camp: Spread mustard onto one side of each biscuit. Wrap each cocktail wiener in a *half* of a biscuit. Place the wrapped weiners into two prepared foil cake pans and cover each pan with a second pan turned upside down and secure. Place the pans on a rack over the keyhole fire pit and cook turning each smokie wrap ¼ turn every 5 minutes for a total of 20 minutes or until the biscuits are done. Dip in barbeque sauce.
Serves 4

Pizza Potatoes

1-10 ounce package dehydrated scalloped potatoes
1-4 ounce pkg sliced pepperoni
4 ounces shredded mozzarella cheese
1-15 ounce jar pizza sauce
2 Tablespoons margarine divided
1 Tablespoon Italian seasoning
1 teaspoon salt
¼ teaspoon pepper

At camp: Soak the dehydrated potatoes for at least four hours in a large re-closeable bag in enough water to cover the potatoes. Drain off the water gently squeezing as much water out as possible. Melt 1 Tablespoon of margarine in each of two prepared foil cake pans placed on a rack over the keyhole fire pit. Place half of the potatoes in each pan and sprinkle each with ½ Tablespoon Italian seasoning, ½ teaspoon salt and 1/8 teaspoon pepper. Cook turning occasionally until potatoes are browned. Remove the pan from the heat and stir ½ of the pizza sauce into each pan. Top each pan of ingredients with ½ of the pepperoni and 2 ounces of the shredded mozzarella cheese. Cover each pan with a second pan turned upside down and secure. Cook until cheese is bubbly approximately 15 minutes.
Serves 4

Scalloped Ham 'n Potatoes

1 package dehydrated scalloped potatoes
8 ounces cubed ham
1-10 ounce can cream of mushroom soup
2 Tablespoons oil
4 ounces shredded cheddar cheese
½ cup milk
1 teaspoon Worcestershire sauce
Seasoning packet included with potatoes

At camp: Soak the dehydrated potatoes in a large re-closeable bag for at least four hours and drain. Place 1 Tablespoon of oil in each of two prepared foil pans. Stir in the potatoes, seasoning packet, soup, milk, Worcestershire sauce and ham. Top with the shredded cheese and cover with a second pan turned upside down and secure. Cook on a rack over the keyhole fire for 25 minutes or until bubbly and cheese is melted.
Serves 4

Ham and Broccoli Bake

1-16 ounce package frozen chopped broccoli
2 cups cubed ham
3 ounces French fried onion rings
1 cup shredded cheddar cheese
1-10 ounce can cream of mushroom soup
¼ cup milk
1 teaspoon Worcestershire sauce

At camp: Place the thawed broccoli into a prepared foil pan with enough water to cover the broccoli. Cook on a rack over the keyhole fire pit until the broccoli is tender. *Do not let it boil dry.* Drain off the liquid and stir in the condensed soup, milk, Worcestershire sauce, ham and half of the onion rings. Top with the shredded cheddar cheese and the remaining onion rings. Cover the pan with a second pan turned upside down and secure. Place the pan onto a rack over the keyhole fire pit adding a small scoop of hot coals to create an even temperature and cook for 20 minutes or until heated through. Let stand 5 minutes.
Tip: Green beans can be substituted for the broccoli.
Serves 4

Pan Pizza

2 cups biscuit mix
½ cup water
1 teaspoon oregano
1 teaspoon Italian seasoning
½ cup pizza sauce
1-4 ounce package pepperoni slices
4 ounces shredded mozzarella cheese
2 Tablespoons olive oil

At camp: Prepare two foil cake pans. Rub each pan with 1 Tablespoon of olive oil. In a large re-closeable bag mix the biscuit mix, oregano, Italian seasoning and water until smooth. Divide the dough in half and press each half into a pan prepared with olive oil. Place both pans on a rack over the keyhole fire pit uncovered. Cook for 5 to 7 minutes or until dough is set but not browned. Turn the dough over and spread half of the pizza sauce over each crust using about ¼ cup per crust. Top each pizza with half of the shredded cheese and then half of the pepperoni or optional toppings. Cover both pans with a second pan turned upside down and secure.Cook on a rack over the keyhole fire pit for 20 to 25 minutes or until the cheese is melted and bubbly. *Placing toppings on the crust to thick will cause an undercooked dough.*

Serves 4

Time saver: Two cans of buttermilk biscuits or canned pizza crust can be used instead of biscuit mix. Press into pan and cook as instructed above.

Optional toppings: Canadian bacon, ½ lb cooked ground beef, ½ lb cooked sausage, 1-4oz can drained sliced olives, 1-4oz can drained mushrooms, chopped green bell peppers, chopped onions.

Cheesy Potatoes

1 cup dehydrated hash browns
1 teaspoon salt
½ cup real bacon bits
2 cups shredded cheddar cheese
2 Tablespoons margarine
1 cup sour cream
½ cup milk
1-10 ounce can condensed cream of celery soup
1 cup dry fine bread crumbs

At camp: Prepare one foil cake pan. Soak the hash browns in a gallon sized re-closeable bag in just enough water to cover for 3 hours or until soft and drain. Melt the margarine in a prepared foil cake pan. Add the drained hash browns, bacon bits, cheese, and salt and mix well. In a medium sized plastic bag mix the sour cream, soup and milk together and pour the mixture over the potato mixture. Top with dry bread crumbs if desired. Cover the pan with a second pan turned upside down and secure. Place the pan on a rack over the keyhole fire pit and cook for 45 minutes or until set.
Serves 4

Pineapple Upside Down Cake

1-9 ounce single layer yellow cake mix
1 egg
½ cup water
½ cup brown sugar
¼ cup margarine
1-8 ounce can pineapple slices drained
whipped topping

Prepare ahead: Place the egg and the water into a medium sized re-closeable bag and seal.

At camp: Add the cake mix to the egg and the water in a gallon sized re-closeable bag. Seal the bag and shake it to mix the ingredients thoroughly. Melt the margarine in one prepared foil cake pan on a rack over the keyhole fire pit. Stir the brown sugar into the melted margarine and arrange the drained pineapple slices over the brown sugar and margarine mixture. Pour the prepared cake mix over the top of the pineapple slices. Cover the pan with a second pan turned upside down and secure. Cook on a rack over the keyhole fire pit placing a small scoop of hot coals on the top pan to create an even temperature for 20 to 25 minutes or until the cake is done. Turn the pan over with the cake inside to invert the cake. Serve warm with whipped topping.

Serves 4

Cherry Chocolate Cake

1-9 ounce single layer size chocolate cake mix
1 egg
½ cup water
1-21 oune can cherry pie filling
whipped topping

Prepare ahead: Place the egg and the water into a medium sized re-closeable bag and seal.

At camp: Add the cake mix to the egg and water in the bag and seal. Shake the bag to mix the contents. Pour the can of cherry pie filling into one prepared foil cake pan and cover it with the prepared cake mix. Cover the pan with a second pan turned upside down and secure. Cook it on a rack over the keyhole fire pit placing a small scoop of hot coals on the top pan to create an even temperature for 25 to 30 minutes or until the cake is done in the center. Turn the cake pan over with the cake inside invert the cake. Serve warm with whipped topping.
Serves 4

Apple Gingerbread

½-16 ounce gingerbread mix
1 egg
½ cup water
1-15 ounce can apple pie filling
whipped topping

Prepare ahead: Place the egg, water and pie filling into a gallon sized re-closeable bag and seal.
At camp: Add the gingerbread mix to the ingredients in the bag. Seal the bag and shake it to mix the ingredients. Pour the ingredients into one prepared foil cake pan. Cover the pan with a second pan turned upside down and secure. Cook on a rack over the keyhole fire pit placing a small scoop of hot coals on the top pan to create an even temperature for 30 minutes or until the gingerbread is done. Serve warm with whipped topping.
Serves 4

Apple Crisp

1-21 ounce can apple pie filling
½ teaspoon cinnamon
½ cup margarine
1/3 cup brown sugar
½ cup chopped walnuts
1 cup flour
whipped topping

Prepare ahead: In a medium sized re-closeable bag mix the margarine, brown sugar, cinnamon, walnuts and flour and seal the bag.
At camp: Prepare one foil cake pan. Pour pie filling into prepared pan and sprinkle with the sugar and flour mixture. Cover with a second pan turned upside down and secure. Cook on a rack over the keyhole fire pit placing a small scoop of hot coals on the top pan to create an even temperature for 25 minutes or until top is lightly browned. Serve warm with whipped topping.
Serves 4

Fruit Cobbler

1-15 ounce can fruit pie filling any kind
1 egg
1-7 ounce cake mix any flavor
½ cup water
½ cup brown sugar
whipped topping

At camp: In a large re-closeable bag mix the egg, water and cake mix until well blended. Empty the pie filling into one prepared foil cake pan. Pour the prepared cake mix over the pie filling and sprinkle with brown sugar. Cover with a second pan turned upside down and secure. Cook on a rack over the keyhole fire pit placing a small scoop of hot coals on the top pan to create an even temperature for 30 to 45 minutes or until the cake is done. Serve warm with whipped topping. **Serves 4**

Chapter Six
Cooking on a Stick

Putting a twist to the standard roasted hot dog can be fun for everyone so get them all involved!!

Turkey Bacon Wrap page 116

The Basic Hot Dog

Thread each hot dog onto a stick lengthwise and cook holding approximately 3" above the hot coals turning when it starts to bubble and is browned. Continue cooking until the hot dogs are browned on all sides. Serve on a bun with desired condiments.

Bacon Cheese Dogs

1 package of 8 hot dogs
8 slices bacon
4 slices American cheese

Thread each hot dog onto a stick lengthwise and roast like a basic hot dog as instructed above. Cut a shallow slit lengthwise in the hot dogs not quite to the stick. Place one half of a slice of cheese into each slit. Wrap each hot dog tightly with a piece of bacon in a spiral fashion making sure to slightly overlap the bacon as you go securing the bacon to the hot dog with tooth picks. Hold the bacon wrapped hot dog approximately 2" above the hot coals and roast turning as the bacon gets brown and crispy. Remove the tooth picks and serve in a bun with desired condiments.
Serves 4

Dog in a Biscuit

1 package of 8 hot dogs
2 cans refrigerated biscuit dough

Thread each hot dog onto a stick lengthwise and roast them. Work the biscuit dough in your hands to make it a little warmer and to soften it a little bit. While the hot dog is still on the stick wrap each one in a spiral fashion with two biscuits pinching the seams together thightly. Cook holding approximately 5" above the hot coals turning as the biscuit browns.
Tip: Holding the biscuit too close to the coals will result in a brown crust and a raw middle so have patience...it's worth the time.
Serves 4

Sausage Corn Dogs

1 package of 8 fully cooked smoked sausages
2 cans of refrigerated corn bread stick dough

Roast the sausages using the same instructions as for a hot dog. While the sausage is still on a stick wrap each one in a spiral fashion with two pieces of corn bread stick dough pinching the seams together tightly. Cook holding approximately 5" above the hot coals turning as the dough browns.
Serves 4

Chili Corn Dog

1 package of 8 hot dogs
1-15 ounce can chili
2 cans refrigerated corn bread stick dough
2 cups shredded cheddar cheese

Roast the hot dogs on the stick. Remove the label from the chili and open the can and stir it in the can. Place the opened can directly into the hot coals stirring frequently until heated through. Meanwhile in a spiral fashion wrap each hot dog with two corn bread stick dough pieces pinching the seams together tightly. Cook holding approximately 5" above the hot coals turning as the dough browns. Place the corn dogs on a plate and cover with hot chili and top with shredded cheddar cheese.
Serves 4

Broiled Ham 'n Cheese

8 slices ham lunch meat
2 cans refrigerated crescent roll dough
8 slices Swiss cheese

Wrap each slice of ham tightly around a stick. Wrap each slice of ham with a slice of Swiss cheese. In a spiral fashion wrap each ham and cheese slices on the sticks with two raw crescent rolls pinching the seams together tightly. Cook holding approximately 5" above the hot coals turning as the crescent rolls brown. Pinching the end of the sandwich towards the handle of the stick to keep all the ingredients together slide the sandwich from the stick.
Serves 4

Turkey Bacon Wraps

8 slices turkey lunch meat
2 cans refrigerated crescent roll dough
8 slices bacon
8 slices American cheese

Thread the bacon pieces accordion style onto sticks and cook holding approximately 2" above hot coals until the bacon is done. Wiggle the ends of the cooked bacon pieces to release them from the sticks. Wrap each piece of bacon with a slice of American cheese and then wrap the cheese tightly with a piece of turkey lunch meat. Wrap the bacon, turkey and cheese in a spiral fashion with two raw crescent rolls pinching dough tightly. Cook holding approximately 5" above the hot coals turning as the crescents brown. Pinching the end of the sandwich towards the handle of the stick to keep all the ingredients together slide the sandwich from the stick.
Serves 4

Cheese Sticks

8 string cheese
2 cans refrigerated corn bread sticks
1-15 ounce can marinara sauce

Remove the label from the can of marinara sauce and open the can. Place the can of marinara upright directly into the hot coals stirring the contents occasionally until heated through. Meanwhile thread the string cheese onto sticks lengthwise. Wrap each string cheese with two raw corn bread sticks in a spiral fashion pinching the seams together tightly. Cook holding approximately 5" above the hot coals turning as the dough browns. Pinching the end toward the handle of the stick slide the cheese sticks from the roasting stick. Dip in marinara.
Serves 4

Cinnamon Twists

1 can refrigerated cinnamon roll dough with icing included
sugar and cinnamon mixture

At camp: Wrap each strip of cinnamon roll dough around a roasting
stick in a spiral fashion pinching ends and seams together tightly to
hold together. Sprinkle with extra cinnamon and sugar if desired.
Cook holding approximately 5"above the hot coals turning as the
dough browns. When the dough is done remove it from the sticks and
drizzle the packaged icing over the twists.
Serves 4

Biscuits

Canned refrigerated biscuits any type

Wrap each biscuit in a spiral fashion around the end of a stick
pinching the seams together tightly as you go to keep it on the stick.
Cook holding approximately 5" above the hot coals turning as the
dough browns.

Surf n Turf Stick-ka-Bobs

1 pound sirloin steak ½" thick
1 pound medium sized cooked shrimp
1 green bell pepper
Creole seasoning

Prepare ahead: Trim the fat from the edges of the steak and cut into 1½" cubes and sprinkle with creole seasoning. Seal in a re-closeable plastic bag. Sprinkle the shrimp with creole seasoning and place it into a separate re-closeable bag and seal.
At camp: Cut the bell pepper into 1½" pieces. Thread the food on the sticks in the order given: steak, pepper, and shrimp ending with the steak. Cook holding approximately 4" to 6" above the hot coals turning as necessary until meat is done.
Serves 4

Teriyaki Stick-ka-Bobs

1 pound sirloin steak or 2 boneless skinless chicken breasts
8 ounces fresh whole mushrooms
1 bottle teriyaki sauce
1 green bell pepper

Prepare ahead: Cut the meat into 1½" pieces and place into a gallon size re-closeable bag. Pour the teriyaki sauce over the meat and seal the bag.
At camp: Wash the mushrooms and cut the bell pepper into 1½" pieces. Thread the ingredients onto sticks in the order given: meat, mushroom, pepper. Repeat ending with the meat. Brush everything with any leftover teriyaki sauce. Cook holding approximately 4" to 6" above the hot coals turning as necessary and basting with the teriyaki sauce occasionally until meat is done.
Serves 4

Italian Chicken Stick-ka-Bobs

2 large boneless skinless chicken breasts
1 green bell pepper
4 small red potatoes
1-8 ounce bottle Italian salad dressing
parmesan cheese

Prepare ahead: Cut the chicken into 1½" pieces and place them into a re-closeable bag. Pour the Italian dressing over the chicken and seal the bag. Pierce a small hole in each potato. Microwave the potatoes on high until *partially* cooked. Place into a re-closeable bag and seal the bag.

At camp: Cut the potatoes into 1" pieces and the bell pepper into 1½" pieces and thread the ingredients onto sticks in the order given: chicken, potato, pepper and repeat ending with the meat. Baste with the remaining dressing. Cook holding approximately 4" to 6" above the hot coals turning as necessary until the chicken is done. Sprinkle with parmesan.
Serves 4

Hawaiian Stick-ka-Bobs

1 pound ham cut into 1" cubes
1-15 ounce can pineapple chunks in juice
1 cup tiny tomatoes
1-8 ounce package small whole mushrooms
¼ cup brown sugar

At camp: Drain the can of pineapple chunks reserving ½ cup of the juice. Thread the ingredients onto sticks in the order given: ham, tomato, pineapple and repeat ending with the ham. Mix the reserved pineapple juice and the brown sugar together in a small re-closeable bag and brush onto stick-ka-bobs. Cook holding approximately 4" to 6" above the hot coals turning as necessary and brushing occasionally with the pineapple juice mixture until the meat is done and the vegetables are tender.
Serves 4

Bacon or Breakfast Sausage Links

Sliced bacon or brown and serve sausage links

Sausage link: Thread each sausage link onto a stick lengthwise and roast as instructed for the basic hot dog until golden brown on all sides.
Bacon: Thread each slice of bacon onto a stick in an accordion fashion and roast holding approximately 2" above the hot coals until bacon is browned on both sides.

Smores

8 regular size marshmallows
4-1½ ounce chocolate bars
8 graham crackers

At camp: Break all of the graham crackers in half. Place half of a candy bar on one half of a graham cracker. Roast the marshmallows on a stick over the hot coals holding about 5" above the hot coals until golden brown. Pull the marshmallow from the end of the stick using a half of a graham cracker on the top and a half of a graham cracker with the chocolate on the bottom.
Makes 8

Chapter Seven
Other Methods

Here is a collection of recipes that lighten the chores on that first day at camp when you don't have the time or you are just too tired to cook after traveling and setting up the camp.

Chili Chip Salad page 126

Chili Chip Salad

2 -15 ounce cans chili
1-10 ounce bag corn chips
2 cups shredded lettuce
2 cups shredded cheddar cheese
2 diced tomatoes
Sour cream

Prepare ahead: Shred the lettuce and seal it in a plastic bag. Wrap the lettuce as instructed in chapter two. Chop the tomatoes and seal them in a smaller separate bag.
At camp: Remove the labels from the cans of chili and open. Set the cans of chili upright directly into the hot coals. Carefully stir the chili occasionally using a teaspoon or knife bringing the bottom of the contents to the top as you stir. When the chili is heated through and bubbly remove it from the heat. Place a large hand full of corn chips (about 1½ cups) on each of four plates. Spoon a thin layer of chili over the top of the corn chips on each plate. Top each of the plates with ½ cup shredded lettuce, tomatoes, ½ cup shredded cheese and sour cream.
Optional additional toppings: sliced drained olives, chopped green onion, chopped bell peppers, sliced jalapeño peppers, sliced avocado, and salsa.
Serves 4

Chicken Salad Sandwiches

1 2/3 cups finely chopped cooked chicken
½ cup real mayonnaise
¼ teaspoon onion powder
2 Tablespoons finely chopped onion
¼ teaspoon seasoned salt
2 Tablespoons finely chopped celery
¼ teaspoon garlic powder
8 -1½" thick slices French bread

Prepare ahead: Mix all of the ingredients together except the bread. Put into a re-closeable bag and seal the bag.
At camp: Spread about ½ cup of the chicken mixture on each of four slices of French bread. Top the sandwiches with a second piece of French bread.
Tip: Chicken Salad can be served with crackers and sliced cheese for a snack too.
Serves 4

Smoked Salmon Spinners

2 cups fully cooked smoked salmon cut into chunks
8 ounces softened cream cheese any flavor
3 Tablespoons sour cream
1 Tablespoon milk
1 teaspoon onion powder
1 teaspoon lemon juice
¼ teaspoon salt
8-10" flour tortillas
2 cups shredded smoked cheddar cheese
½ teaspoon liquid smoke

Prepare ahead: Combine the cream cheese, sour cream, milk, lemon juice, liquid smoke, onion powder, and salt. Blend well. Stir in salmon chunks. Seal in a re-closeable bag.
At camp: Spread ¼ cup of the salmon mixture onto each tortilla and top with ¼ cup shredded cheese. Roll up tightly. Slice diagonally into 1" to 2" slices.
Serves 4

Crab Salad Wraps

1-1 pound container crab salad
4-10" tortillas
8 slices individually wrapped American cheese or shredded cheddar

At camp: Place two pieces of American cheese on each tortilla. Spoon ½ cup of the crab salad on the top of the cheese slices and roll up tortilla. Slice if desired or eat as is.
Serves 4

Peanut Butter Banana Wraps

4-10" flour tortillas
4 bananas
1 cup Peanut butter
¼ cup honey

Prepare ahead: Mix the peanut butter with the honey and place it into a small re-closeable bag and seal the bag.
At camp: Spread each tortilla with peanut butter mixture. Place a peeled banana on the tortilla and roll it up. Slice or eat as is.
Serves 4

Speedy Enchiladas

4-15 ounce cans chili
2 cups shredded cheddar cheese
8-8" soft corn tortillas
sour cream
hot sauce

At camp: Remove the labels from the cans of chili and open. Place each can of chili upright directly into the hot coals. Cook stirring frequently with a small spoon or knife bringing the contents from the bottom to the top of the can until the chili is heated through. To assemble place two soft corn tortillas on each of four plates. Sprinkle ¼ cup shredded cheddar cheese down the middle of each tortilla and cover cheese on each tortilla with approximately ¼ cup chili. Roll the tortilla up turning to place the seam on the bottom. Cover each filled tortilla with the extra chili. Serve with sour cream and hot sauce.
Serves 4

Beef Dips

12 deli style slices beef roast lunch meat
4 hoagie or kaiser rolls
2-10 ounce cans condensed beef broth
2 Tablespoons browning & seasoning sauce

At camp: Remove the labels from the condensed broth and open the cans. Add 1 Tablespoon of the browning and seasoning sauce to each can of broth and place them upright directly into the hot coals. Cook stirring frequently until heated through. Pile the beef slices onto the hoagie or kaiser rolls. Pour a half of a can of broth each into 4 small bowls. Dip the sandwiches into the broth as you are eating them. **Serves 4**

Mile High Hoagies

1 loaf French bread
¼ cup mayonnaise
6 slices Swiss cheese
6 thin slices ham
6 slices American cheese
1-4 ounce package sliced pepperoni
6 thin slices turkey
1 thinly sliced cucumber
1-4 ounce can sliced olives
½ thinly sliced green bell pepper
lettuce
Mustard (optional)
Parmesan cheese (optional)

At camp: Cut the bread open in half length wise. Spread each side of the bread with the mayonnaise and the mustard if desired. Place the ingredients on the bread in the order given: the ham slices, the turkey slices, American cheese slices, Swiss cheese slices, pepperoni, cucumber, bell pepper, olives and lettuce. Top with parmesan cheese if desired. Close the loaf and cut the sandwich into four large pieces.
Serves 4

Fresh Vegetable Salad

1 cup fresh broccoli florets
1 cup fresh baby carrots
1 cup fresh cauliflower florets
1 cup fresh cucumber slices
½ cup green bell pepper strips
1-4oz can drained sliced olives
1-8oz bottle ranch salad dressing
2 cups cubed cooked ham

Prepare ahead: Wash all of the vegetables and cut them into bite sized pieces. In a gallon sized re-closeable bag mix all of the ingredients and seal the bag.
At camp: Serve right out of the bag with slices of French bread on the side.
Serves 4

Ham Spinwheels

8 slices ham lunch meat
soft cream cheese
4 green onions
fresh crab meat

Prepare ahead: Spread each ham slice with a thin layer of room temperature cream cheese. Trim the white end off from the green onions. Place the green stem of the onions on four of the ham slices and roll them up tightly from the narrow end. Place a row of crab meat on the remaining four ham slices and roll up tightly from the narrow end. Place all of the ham rolls into a large re-closeable bag and seal.
At camp: Slice each ham roll across into 6 slices and serve.
Makes 48

Crunchy Chicken Salad

2 cups cubed cooked chicken
½ cup diced celery
½ cup mayonnaise
¼ cup minced onion
1 teaspoon garlic powder
1 teaspoon celery salt
1-4 ounce can sliced olives
1-4 ounce can shoestring potato chips
1 cup fresh red grapes
2 small cantaloupes

Prepare ahead: Combine the cubed chicken, mayonnaise, celery, onion, garlic powder, celery salt and drained olives. Seal in a recloseable bag.
At camp: Stir the shoestring potato chips into the chicken salad mixture. Cut the cantaloupes in half accross the short side and scoop out all of the seeds. Fill each cantaloupe half with ¼ of the chicken salad.
Serves 4

Make Ahead Hot Cocoa Mix

2 ¼ cups sugar
1 ½ cups powdered coffee creamer
1 teaspoon salt
1 ¼ cup unsweetened baking cocoa
5 ½ cups powdered milk
marshmallows

Prepare ahead: Mix all of the ingredients in a large re-closeable bag and seal.
At camp: Stir ¼ cup mix into one mug of hot water for each serving. Top with marshmallows.

Make Ahead Mocha Mix

2 cups powdered vanilla coffee creamer
1¾ cups sugar
¾ cup instant coffee granules
¾ cup unsweetened baking cocoa
½ teaspoon salt
whipped topping

Prepare ahead: Mix all of the ingredients in a large re-closeable bag and seal.
At camp: Stir ¼ cup of the mocha mix to one mug hot water. Top with whipped topping.
Tip: Hazelnut or amaretto coffee creamer can be used in place of the vanilla coffee creamer.

Boiled Eggs

4 eggs
4 wax coated 6 ounce paper cups

At camp: Place each whole egg into a wax coated paper cup. Fill each cup to the top with water. Set the filled cups upright directly into the hot coals. *The cup will not burn below the water level.* Cook for approximately 30 minutes replenishing the water as needed to keep the water from dissipating.
Makes 4

Caramel Banana Cake

2 bananas
1-12 ounce jar caramel ice cream topping
½ lb frozen chocolate pound cake
whipped topping

At camp: Cut the thawed cake into 4 slices. Place each of the slices onto plates. Slice the bananas and place them onto each slice of cake. Drizzle the caramel topping over the bananas and cake slices. Top with whipped topping.
Serves 4

Chocolate Dessert Sandwiches

1-1 pound frozen chocolate cake
1 can ready to spread chocolate frosting
1-12 ounce jar chocolate syrup
whipped topping

At Camp: Slice the cake into 8 slices and place four slices on plates. Spread each cake slice on the plates with the frosting and cover with a second slice of cake. Drizzle with choclate syrup. Top with whipped topping.
Variations: Any available flavor cake, frosting and topping can be used. Sprinkle with decorative cake candies or chopped nuts.
Serves 4

Index

A

B

C

Chicken

G

H

I

L

M

T

Printed in the United Kingdom
by Lightning Source UK Ltd.
132023UK00001BA/10/A